introduction

This booklet is only intended as a starting point, and, whilst it is hoped that the student will gain a serious insight into the craft, further reading on the subject is thoroughly recommended. To this end a list of books is included at the back of the pamphlet. Five basic alphabets are illustrated, as well as short pieces on the history of writing, how to use the pen, design and layout, and a few pieces of work by leading practitioners of the craft.

The qualities which should be aimed towards in calligraphy are those of rhythm, spontaneity, sharpness, and clarity. Rhythm will come as spacing begins to get more even; spontaneity is the product of complete familiarity with the style being used; sharpness, good definition between thick and thin strokes, will occur as one becomes better acquainted with the tools; and clarity is the ease with which a piece can be read. It is very important that these disciplines should be mastered before moving on to the freer, more self-expressive aspects of writing. Attention must always be paid to margins because an attractive piece of writing can be ruined if the margins are not sympathetic to the work. More will be said about that in the section dealing with layout.

a brief history of writing

When one considers that writing has been so important in the communication of history, very little is actually known about the early history of writing. It had originally been thought that the alphabet, as we know it, had developed directly from the hieroglyphs, and hieratic & demotic scripts of ancient Egypt. However, it seems more likely that writing developed from makers' marks on various artifacts made in the Mediterranean area at the dawn of civilization and was influenced by the Egyptians.

The first recognizable alphabetic script probably evolved with the Western Semites about 1600 BC. From there it was improved by the Phoenicians, who, sailing out of Tyre and Sidon carried its influence over the whole of the then known world.

Of the two different alphabets in use in Phoenicia, the Moabite or Tyrian, and the Sidonian, it was the Sidonian which formed the basis for the Greek alphabet which began to take shape sometime about 1000 to 900 BC, reaching its zenith between 500 and 300 BC.

The Roman alphabet, like the rest of its civiliza-

IMP·CAESARI·DIVI·NERVAE·F·NERVAE
TRAIANO·AVG·GERM·DACICO·PONTIF
MAXIMO·TRIB·POT·XVII·IMP·VI·COS·VI·P·P

a. Part of a cast of an inscription on the Trajan Column in Rome: A·D·113. Victoria & Albert Museum, London.

tion, was very strongly influenced by the
Etruscans, who migrated to Italy from Asia
Minor via Egypt and Carthage, absorbing
much of the Greek culture on the way. The
Romans, having already adopted a lot of the
Etruscan culture, finally conquered them at the
battle of Cumae in 281 BC.

The design of the Roman alphabet progressed
slowly but steadily over the next three hundred
years reaching its apogee with the inscription
on the Trajan column, constructed at the end
of the 1st Century AD. At the same time that in-
scriptional lettering was developing there were
two written hands in use – the Roman Square
Capitals (Capitalis Quadrata) and the cursive.
The style known as Rustic Capitals (Capitalis
Rustica) gradually began to come into use,
being a more freely written letter, and was used
as an initial letter in manuscripts as late as
the 11th Century.

There appears to have been a rather abrupt
change in style to the Uncial letter at about
the time that Constantine adopted Christianity,
a style that had been in use in Greece as early

a. Part of Virgil's Georgics:
   Roman Quadrata Capitals, 4th Century.
   From H. Degering - Lettering
b. Part of Virgil's Aeneid, Codex Palatinus.
   Roman Rustic Capitals, 4th Century.
   Vatican Library.

as the 3rd Century B.C. It has been suggested that this was a deliberate political decision, i.e. not to use a style of writing that was associated with the oppressors of the early Christians. The Uncial derived its name from having been written an "uncia" (a Roman inch) in height.

Originally written with a slanted pen, the flat pen style of the Greeks was adopted in about the 6th Century.

A version of Half Uncials was found to have been written in Rome as early as the 4th Century, but they really evolved after the 6th Century in Ireland under the influence of what was being taught in Iona. Although Christianity spread outwards from Rome, it was in the areas on the fringe of the Empire where Christianity, and with it writing, really flourished after the fall of Rome. Iona was a religious and cultural center, where many of the scholars of the day were trained. These men would then have re-

DEUOTI AFFECTUS
PIGNORA MITTO MEI
MEQUE MEOSQ·OPTANS
TANTI INTERCAUDIA PATRIS
INCAELIS MEMOREM

AMBULABAT APUD IUDAEOS
SED ABIIT IN REGIONEM IUXTA·
DESERTUM INCIUITATEM
QUAE DICITUR EFREM
ET IBI MORABATUR CUM DISCIP SUIS
PROXIMUM AUTEM ERAT
PASCHA IUDAEORUM

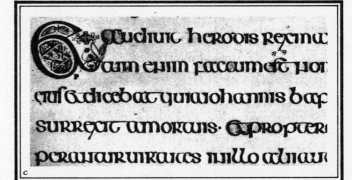

a. Part of dedicatory page of Codex Amiatinus
Uncials, written at Wearmouth-Jarrow, late 7th Century.
Biblioteca Laurenziana, Florence.
b. From 'The Gospel of St·John'
Uncials, written at Wearmouth-Jarrow, 7th Century.
Library of Stonyhurst College, England.

c. From the 'Book of Kells'
Irish Half-Uncials c. A·D· 800.
Trinity College, Dublin.

part, for the similarity between such books as the Book of Kells, the Book of Durrow, and the Lindisfarne Gospels – supreme examples of the art of the times.

At the same time that the Uncials and Half Uncials were in use in the British Isles, various other styles were developing throughout the rest of Europe. In the South of England, the Anglo-Saxons introduced two runic characters to make the sounds "th" (thorn) and "w". In France, Merovingian and East Frankish writing were in use, whilst in Italy, Visigothic or the Old Italian style was developing.

In the 8th Century, Charlemagne became ruler of the Holy Roman Empire, and at this time came the first attempt since the fall of Rome to establish a standard hand throughout

turned to their own areas, taking their acquired skills with them. This probably accounts, in some

a. Part of the Lindisfarne Gospels
   English Half-Uncials, late 7th Century.
   British Museum, London.

b. Part of Bede's 'Historia Ecclesiastica Gentis Anglorum'.
   Anglo-Saxon minuscule, 8th Century.
   British Museum, London.

Western Europe. A decree was issued (probably due in no small part to the influence of Alcuin of York) in 789 to the effect that all hands were to be standardized. It has been thought by some that Alcuin was responsible for the remodelling of this hand but this is far from proven.

The minuscule letter as we know it, finally evolved with the introduction of the Carolingian hand. It had great charm and beauty, and was written with extreme freedom.

One of the writing centres employing the Carolingian hand was Winchester in England and the style which had developed there by the 10th Century is thought by many to be the most beautiful. It was this hand which Edward Johnston took as his model for the basic foundational hand.

Throughout history one art form has tended to be influenced by another, and writing is no different in this respect. As the rounded Roman and Norman arches in architecture began to give way to the taller, pointed arch, so letters started to become compressed and more pointed.

sullimiores animę quę uiri
ac mulieris copulam fasti
dirent conubium concu

The influence of gothic form began to be felt from about the 12th Century, reaching its height in the late 14th and early 15th Centuries. The Gothic movement was almost entirely a feature of Northern Europe and its influence was little felt in the Mediterranean countries. During this period, the main producers of manuscripts changed from the monastic centers to the to the specialist craft workshops supervised by the guilds.

The humanist scribes of the Renaissance developed their "cursiva humanista" directly from the Carolingian minuscule. From this resulted a slightly faster and more compressed style which had more "spring" and life to it - "cancellaresca" or italic writing.

a. English Pontifical
   Transitional period between Carolingian & Gothic, 12th Century.
   British Museum, London.

b. French Psalter
   Gothic, late 13th Century.
   Fitzwilliam Museum, Cambridge, England.
c. Cursiva humanista
   Ciriagio of Florence 1454
   British Museum, London.

At the time that the scribes were perfecting
their humanist styles in Italy, Gutenberg was
working on his invention of movable type.
Rarely in history, let alone the history of gra-
phics and communication, has one man had
such a profound influence on the course of events
in his own field. The work of the scribe as a pure
copyist began to change and he was forced to
seek work in the realms of law, commerce,
teaching and diplomacy where writing skills
were at a premium. The illuminators went their
separate way, employed mainly on decorating
initial letters in spaces left for this purpose in
the texts of typeset books.

a. From 'La Paraphrasi' by Marcantonio Flaminio
   Humanista and cancellaresca (italic), 16th Century.
   British Museum, London.

Despite the introduction of type, there was still
a great interest in writing and the 16th Century
saw the rise of the writing master, producing
books on 'how to do it' – such men as Arrighi,
Tagliente and Palatino.

b. From 'Libro Nuovo' by Giovanbattista Palatino
   Cursiva cancellaresca, 1561.

As the influence of the writing masters began to wane, so the study of letterform began to disintegrate. The art of writing with a broad-edged pen was lost and writing - copperplate - was executed with a quill or a flexible steel pen to reflect the thick and thin strokes as engraved onto a metal plate.

By the end of the 19th Century writing had reached a rather sorry state, being poorly done with rather sloppy letterforms. At this time Edward Johnston, a medical student in rather poor health, was encouraged by William Morris (who had himself tried his hand at calligraphy) and W. R. Lethaby (the then Principal of the Central School of Arts and Crafts in London) to study old manuscripts in an attempt to discover the lost arts of writing.

He spent endless hours at the British Museum studying, first of all, the Half Uncial scripts and then moving on to the Carolingian hands. He recognized that calligraphy, written with a broad-edged pen, achieved its thick and thin strokes by the angle of the pen being kept constant rather than by exerting pressure.

O GOD, who hast prepared for them that love thee such good things as pass man's understanding; Pour into our hearts such love toward thee, that we, loving thee above

In 1906 his book 'Writing and Illuminating and Lettering' was published, still the 'bible' of calligraphers, in which he set down his discoveries on the art of calligraphy and illumination.

His classes at the Central School and later at the Royal College of Art encouraged and developed the skills of his students whose influence is felt throughout the calligraphic world. In this way, it may be said that it is due almost entirely to his efforts that calligraphy is in the healthy, flourishing state that it is today.

a. Collect for 6th Sunday after Trinity
Foundational Hand. Edward Johnston 1919.
Inscribed for Mr. Frank Rinder.

preparation for writing

The tools required will be: a selection of dip pen points, (Brause or Mitchell), a penholder, ink, a pencil, a ruler, a drawing board, a T-square, and a triangle. The ruling of lines and the general setting up of work will be made much easier with these last three.

Sit comfortably at a table in a room where there are likely to be few disturbances. Hold the drawing board at an angle, either resting in the lap against the edge of the table, or else, propped up on the table at a suitable angle. If the eyes are kept vertically above the hand during writing, it will be easier to judge the quality of the letters and the rhythm being achieved. It will be necessary to fix the paper to the board whilst ruling lines, but when actually writing, keep the paper free so that it can be moved in order to be able to write in the same position all the time. Work should always be protected by a separate piece of paper to prevent grease being transferred from hand to work, making it difficult to write towards the foot of the page.

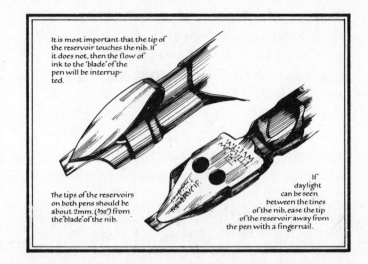

It is most important that the tip of the reservoir touches the nib. If it does not, then the flow of ink to the 'blade' of the pen will be interrupted.

The tips of the reservoirs on both pens should be about 2mm. (³⁄₃₂") from the 'blade' of the nib.

If daylight can be seen between the tines of the nib, ease the tip of the reservoir away from the pen with a fingernail.

The Brause and Mitchell points should be used with detachable reservoirs which are located either on top of or beneath the pen. When the pen is being washed out (which should always be done when work is finished) the reservoir may be removed to facilitate cleaning. To replace the reservoir, simply push it all the way back, so that the tip is about 2mm. from the blade of the pen.

NB. Only a <u>non</u>-waterproof ink should be used. Waterproof Indian inks contain shellac which clogs the pen, making the writing look heavy and rather clumsy.

beginning to write with a broad-edged pen

Most people are familiar with the copperplate (English Round Hand) style of writing, where thick and thin strokes are achieved by exerting pressure on a flexible pen. However, in calligraphy with a broad-edged pen, this is not the case. The thick and thin strokes are caused purely by the shape of the pen and the direction in which it is moved. The pen is held at a constant angle and the exercises shown are intended to familiarize the student with this effect. Different styles of writing will demand different pen angles, but whatever the individual style, the angle will remain constant within it.

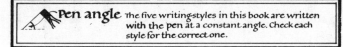

Pen angle The five writing-styles in this book are written with the pen at a constant angle. Check each style for the correct one.

Pen angle refers to the angle which the thin stroke makes to the horizontal line.
Spend some time on these exercises using the largest pen point.

FOUNDATIONAL HAND MINUSCULE

pen angle 30°-35°

a – ascender height 7 pen widths
b – capital height 6 pen widths
c – x height 4 pen widths

Based on a circular o.

ascenders

o abcdefghijkl

The Foundational Hand should be kept as upright as possible. NEVER allow your writing to slope backwards.

The bowl of the g stops short of the bottom line.

counters

mnpqrstuvwxyz

Note that the inner feet of the letters are kept smaller than the outer feet.

descenders   interspaces

The W is like two slightly narrower Vs joined together.

Note the construction of the serif. The round underside should reflect part of a circle.

oabccdefghijklm

These letters are broken down into individual strokes; the numbers and arrows indicate the sequence and direction of those strokes.

These strokes are pushed up out of the vertical stroke. Allow ligatures between letters to happen naturally. Do not force them.

npqrstuvwwxyz

FOUNDATIONAL HAND MAJUSCULE

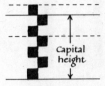

Capital
height

O   These capital letters are based on the
     Monumental Roman Capitals.
     Attempt to keep these proportions.

A B C D E F

Because the pen is held at a constant angle of less than 45°, there
is a difference in weight between the vertical and horizontal strokes.

The pen angle on the vertical strokes of the N can be
steepened a little to lighten their weight.

G H I J K L M N P Q

Keep the finishing stroke on the J
rather small and discreet.

SPACING of capital letters is of paramount importance: equal
areas of counter and interspace will create an inherent rhythm.

R S T U V W X Y Z

The design of ampersands is virtually limitless
in its possibilities. Try designing one of your own.

The traditional up-and-down characteristics
of the numerals need not be adhered to.

& 1 2 3 4 5 6 7 8 9 0

ITALIC HAND MINUSCULE

The Italic Hand is based on a slanting (usually not less than 5° from the vertical) and elliptical O and is NOT just a compressed Roman.

pen angle 45-50°.

a – ascender height 9 pen widths
b – capital height 7 pen widths
c – x height 5 pen widths

Freedom, rhythm and spontaneity are essential in this hand particularly.

o abcdefghijkl

The follow-through of the stroke may cause slight roughness at the end of the letter.

mnpqrstuvwxyz

This hand draws a lot of its character from the way it springs from its roots.

Ligatures will occur between letters when written freely but they should never be forced.

oabccdefghijklmn

These letters are broken down into individual strokes, the numbers and arrows indicating the sequence and direction of these strokes.

The letter y is formed by turning the pen onto its left-hand corner at this point.

Study of the work of Italian writing masters will show the student how to 'swash' or flourish Italic letters. However, it is essential to have a complete grasp of the basics of the letter before going on to attempt these. Only flourish from natural extensions of the letter.

pqrstuvwxyz

ITALIC HAND MAJUSCULE

The capital letters should be slightly more open in character than the minuscule italics.

Capital height.

O ABCDEFG
HIJKLMNPQ

When flourishing these capitals, it should only be done from natural extensions of the letter (see Arrighi, Tagliente, Palatino, etal.).

RSTUVWXYZ

The letters V & W are formed in one stroke.   The crossbar on the Z is not obligatory.

& 1234567890

HALF UNCIAL HAND

a – ascender height 5½ pen widths
b – x height 3½ pen widths

pen angle about 5°.

a b **Ioabcdefghïjklm**

This letter is again based on a circular o, but with the pen held at an almost flat angle, which will be easier to achieve if the elbow is tucked well in.

Note the curve in the vertical strokes of the letters b, l & t.

npqrrstuvwxyz

The serifs are an essential feature of Half-Uncial writing.

oabcdefghïjk

These letters are broken down into individual strokes, the numbers and arrows indicating the sequence and direction of those strokes.

lmnpqrrstu

The thickening strokes indicated here would probably have resulted naturally when written with a quill, simply by exerting a little pressure at the end of the down-stroke.

vwxyz

Although the Uncial letters are shown opposite as possible capital letters to go with the Half-Uncials, this is historically inaccurate. The Half-Uncials developed from the Uncials and probably never appeared together on the same manuscript page. Emphasis would have been given by using a larger, decorative version of the half-uncial.

UNCIAL HAND

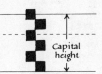

Capital height

The ascender of the d begins almost vertically above
the left-hand edge of the bowl of the letter.

O ABCDDEE

These letters reflect the characteristics of the Roman letter proportions.
The flat pen style is fairly typical of Greek letters of the early Christian era.

Study of early manuscripts is earnestly recommended, to
see and understand the spacing between letters, words & lines.

FGhijklmNp

The letters J, K, V & W were never, and the Y & Z were rarely
seen in the Uncials, so these have been constructed in that style.

Pen manipulation and 'building up' is a real feature of this hand. The finishing on the letters E, F, L & T
are made by taking the pen to the end of the horizontal stroke, lifting the right hand corner and pulling
the left hand corner across and slightly down making a second stroke.

QRSTUVWXYZ

There is no historical precedent for the use of Arabic numerals in the
Uncial Hand. These have been added solely as a guide.

& 1234567890

GOTHIC BLACK LETTER MINUSCULE

The Gothic Hand can create a most beautiful textural pattern because of its insistent vertical strokes. This rhythm can create problems of legibility, so the rhythm must be tempered slightly to make a piece of work easier to read.

a - ascender height 6 pen widths
b - capital height 5 pen widths
c - x height 4 pen widths

pen angle about 40°.

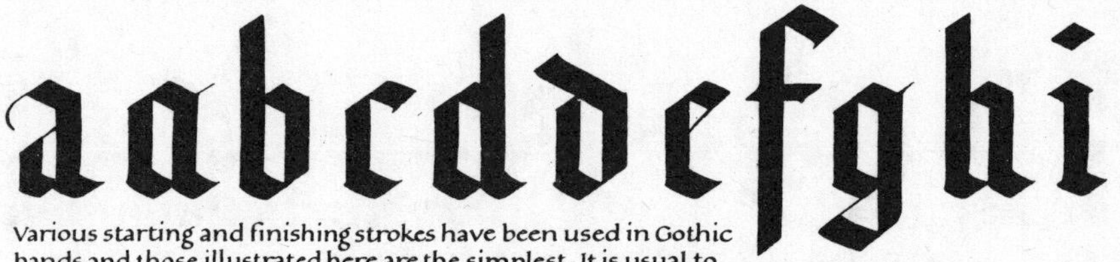

Various starting and finishing strokes have been used in Gothic hands and those illustrated here are the simplest. It is usual to start a letter on a thin stroke, in order to distribute the ink along the blade of the pen. It may be necessary to load a little more ink than normal into the pen to ensure a clean start to the letter.

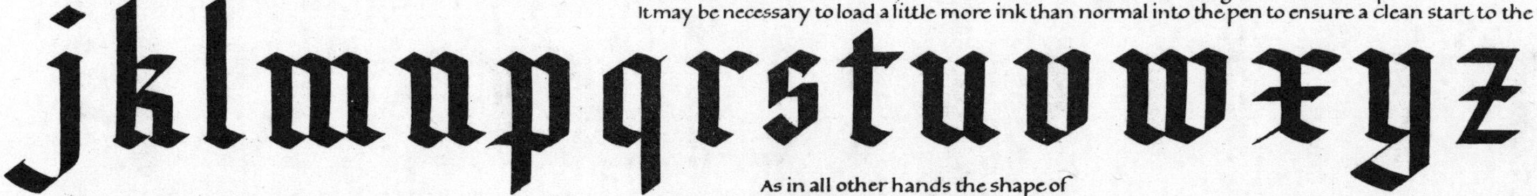

o aabcddefghi

jklmnpqrstuvwxyz

As in all other hands the shape of the O governs the shapes of the rest of the letters.

This stroke is made with the left-hand corner of the pen.

o'aabcddefghijkl

These letters are broken down into individual strokes; the numbers and arrows indicate the sequence and direction of those strokes.

Note that there is a slight tendency to push the stroke back at the foot of the letter.

mnpqrstuvwxyz

GOTHIC BLACK LETTER MAJUSCULE

Capital height

Although intended to be decorative these capitals follow much the same construction rules as other capitals with the decoration being added at the end.

O A B C D E F

The thin strokes are done either with the blade of the pen at 90° to the horizontal, or alternatively by using the corner of the pen.

G H I J K L M N P Q

Try to make as obvious a distinction as possible between the letters C, E & G.

Do not over elaborate these capitals at the expense of legibility.

R S T U V W X Y Z

It is almost impossible to arrive at a successfully designed set of Gothic numerals. These shown here are merely suggestions. The student might consider Roman numerals as an alternative, which was the general answer in the Gothic revival lettering of the nineteenth century.

G 1 2 3 4 5 6 7 8 9 0

RUNNING BOOK HAND MINUSCULE

a – ascender height 7 pen widths
b – capital height 5 pen widths
c – x height 3½ pen widths

pen angle 30°-35°

abc

o abcdefghijklm

These letters, like the Foundational Hand, are based on a circular o, but written more freely and quickly. The hand has its origins in the early 9th Century Carolingian.

npqqrsttuvwxyz

There are no constructed serifs in this hand allowing for greater speed of writing.

Care should be exercised when using the round form of T. It may tend to look like a C.

Unlike the Foundational Hand, many of these letters are done in one stroke.

oabccdefghijklmn

These letters are broken down into individual strokes; the numbers and arrows indicate the sequence and direction of those strokes

The pen should be turned onto its left-hand corner at this point.

pqqrsttuvwxyz

RUNNING BOOK HAND MAJUSCULE

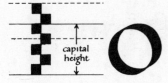

capital height

O

These capitals are again written freely and can also be used to great effect as small capitals in Italic hand done at x height.

Allow plenty of space between letters when writing all capitals.

A B C D E E

Note that the corners at the foot of the letters B, D, E & L are very slightly rounded indicating the speed with which they are written.

F G H I J K L M N P Q

The vertical strokes in the letters B, D, E & F are written first.

R R S T T U V W X Y Z

Note the slight difference in form between the centres of these two letters.

The letters U, V, W & Z are written in one stroke.

& 1 2 3 4 5 6 7 8 9 0

some advice on rhythm and spacing

As was stated earlier, one of the most important aspects of calligraphy is rhythm, which will be acquired as the student becomes better acquainted with his tools and the various writing styles. It would probably be fair to say that a true calligrapher is someone who has ceased to regard the pen as a tool, but rather as an extension of himself. Rhythm itself is achieved through uniformity of writing and spacing. The vertical strokes in the writing should appear to be evenly spaced. The amount of space is governed by the letter itself, or, more correctly, by the size of the counter (the space inside the letter). If the interspace (the space between the letters) is of the same area as the counter, then it will be seen that the rhythm will be even throughout. Thus the space between letters in a foundational hand will be more than that required by, say, a gothic hand.

The rhythm and spacing of capital letters present slightly different problems. Because one

The number of different styles of writing available to the calligrapher is almost limitless. Each of these styles has its own separate rhythm. This example shows the variety of rhythms in the five styles of the book

is constantly faced with the question of compensation for the letters that have gone before and those following, and because one sometimes has the difficulty of juxtaposing letters which form large interspaces, e.g. L and A, or T and T, a larger amount of space is usually required between the letters than would be the case in a minuscule hand. Whereas there are few problems spacing letters with straight, sides, it will be seen from the example that a rounded letter will need to 'cut' the line in order to appear on it. Therefore, when spacing capitals, the decision must be made as to where the vertical line would come to appear evenly spaced, and then to 'cut' it with the rounded or the diagonal letter. As one becomes more experienced so spacing, and rhythm, become automatic.

It is important to allow sufficient space between the lines of writing to allow the eye to read along them. Do not allow "rivers" of white to run vertically through the calligraphy.

LETTERING & CALLIGRAPHY

Capital letters showing the correct areas of space necessary for good rhythm.

LETTERING AND CALLIGRAPHY

In this example the letters have equal distances between their extremities, as would be the case with type, rather than equal areas. This should be avoided.

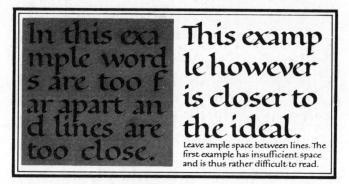

In this example words are too far apart and lines are too close.

This example however is closer to the ideal.

Leave ample space between lines. The first example has insufficient space and is thus rather difficult to read.

This will tend to happen if there is either, too much space between words, or not enough between lines, or a combination of the two.

hints on design and layout

Design and layout are really, like color, governed by one's personal attitudes. There are very
few actual rules regarding design. The important fact to remember is that a piece of work
must have visual impact which can be best
achieved by using contrasting size and weight
of letters and color. The should student make
a study not just of calligraphy, but also of
other fields of art and design in order to understand this better.

Visual impact can also be given by a wise
choice of margins. A simple guide to the esta-
blishment of margins is as follows: divide
the longer side of a page by either 16 or 20
(16 for larger margins, 20 for smaller)
and then use 2 of these units at the top of
the page, 3 units at either side, and 4 at the
the bottom. In the case of a book, the 3 units
should spread across the centre line, i.e. 1½
units on either side. The space that is estab-
lished on the page is then the maximum
writing area.

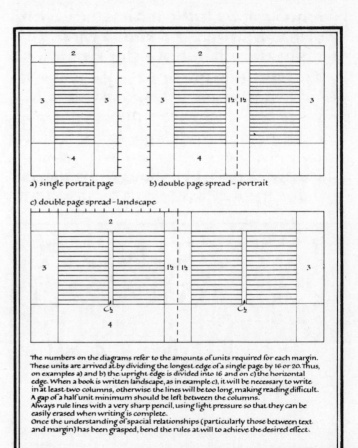

a) single portrait page   b) double page spread - portrait

c) double page spread - landscape

The numbers on the diagrams refer to the amounts of units required for each margin.
These units are arrived at by dividing the longest edge of a single page by 16 or 20. Thus,
on examples a) and b) the upright edge is divided into 16 and on c) the horizontal
edge. When a book is written landscape, as in example c), it will be necessary to write
in at least two columns, otherwise the lines will be too long, making reading difficult.
A gap of a half unit minimum should be left between the columns.
Always rule lines with a very sharp pencil, using light pressure so that they can be
easily erased when writing is complete.
Once the understanding of spacial relationships (particularly those between text
and margin) has been grasped, bend the rules at will to achieve the desired effect.

e likely to be few o

g board at an an

jainst the edge of

o on the table at a

e kept vertically c

riting, it will be e

the letters and th

When writing a piece, the number of words

per line should not exceed 13 or 14, and not be less than 5, with the optimum being 8 or 9. The eye finds it difficult to read very short or very long lines, thus, if one is dealing with a landscape page it might be advisable to put the writing in two columns, as in this booklet. If color is required, colored inks should not be used. They are generally waterproof and translucent, having no "body". Instead, designers' gouache should be used. Mix the required color and then dilute it until a consistency is reached which will flow easily through the pen, but which will not be too watery. It is better, when using color, to write with the board flat, so that there is less chance of the paint flowing to the foot of the letter. When executing calligraphy for reproduction, do the writing twice as large as required on the finished work (twice up) and then have it reduced to size photographically. This will make retouching unnecessary and will retain as much of the spontaneity of the writing as possible. A normal paste-up mechanical can then be made.

conclusion

Calligraphy, like any other art or craft, cannot be learned in a weekend. It requires constant practice. There is a tendency to consider that because one writes already, that calligraphy is just a neater way of handwriting. It is much more than that. It is a very demanding and exacting discipline, to begin with, but great freedom and self expression can develop from it in the future.

In the last twenty years or so, leading calligraphers have attempted to take the craft beyond mere communication (albeit in a very attractive form) and into the realms of fine art. To this end many interesting and exciting things have been happening on both sides of the Atlantic. In Europe, particularly in Britain, the use of traditional tools and methods to approach modern design problems has led to exciting uses of letterforms, gold and color, by such people as Donald Jackson and Ann Hechle. In America, a new approach to calligraphy has been pioneered by Arthur Baker, which involves manipulation of the pen during the construction of a letter. Whilst it is probable that a certain amount of pen manipulating was involved in the writing of Rustic Capitals and Uncials, Arthur Baker's way has been very much more concentrated, resulting in visually exciting letter patterns.

Calligraphy, as something other than a means of communication, as it was before the introduction of movable type, has never been healthier. The upsurge in interest in America, and now in Britain, has meant a demand for teachers far exceeding supply. This calligraphy book is intended to help to bridge that gap.

Calligraphic societies exist in major cities on either side of the Atlantic (the Society of Scribes and Illuminators in London being particularly notable) which foster a love and understanding of calligraphy. Many of these societies run workshops varying in length between one day & two weeks. Membership of one of the societies is recommended.

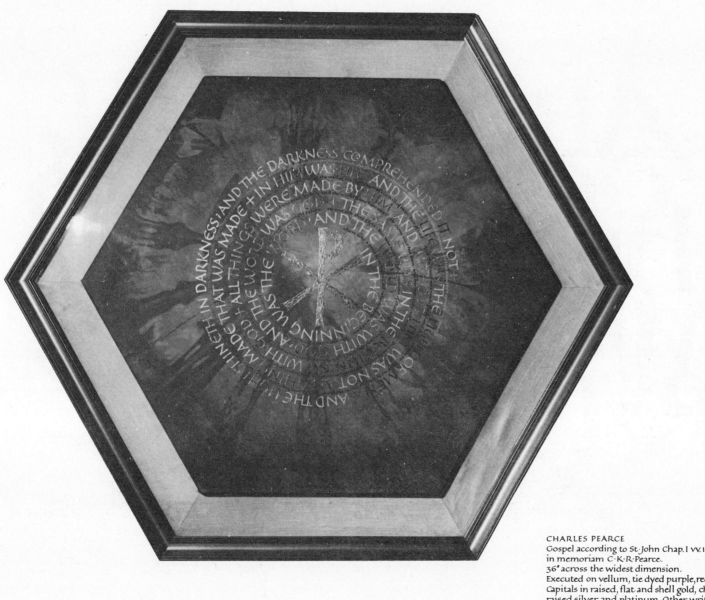

CHARLES PEARCE
Gospel according to St·John Chap. I vv. 1-14,
in memoriam C·K·R·Pearce.
36" across the widest dimension.
Executed on vellum, tie dyed purple, red and blue.
Capitals in raised, flat and shell gold, chrismon in
raised silver and platinum. Other writing in
stick ink and gouache.

ABC
DEFG
HIJKL
MNOPQ
RSTUV
XYZ

Aabcdefg
hijklmn
opqrstuv
vwxyz

ARTHUR BAKER
Two calligraphic alphabets
Written with a Coit pen and reduced
Reproduced by courtesy of Dover Publications.

Within the artwork the following calligraphic text appears:

SEE THE VOICE
SPAKE THAT TO ME

I am Alpha
and Omega the first and the
last
& WHAT YOU
SEE WRITE IN A BOOK

AND GOD
CALLED THE DRY
EARTH: AND THE
GATHERING TOGETHER
OF WATERS
CALLED HE SEAS

DONALD JACKSON
Detail from 'I am the Alpha and Omega'
Height of original – 13"
Executed on vellum in stick ink, raised, flat and
shell gold, and gouache.

The lyf
so short
the craft
so long
to lerne
th'assay
so hard
so sharp
the con
quer
ynge.

Hard
is the herte
that
loveth nought
in May

CHAUCER

GUILLERMO RODRIGUEZ-BENITEZ
Two quotations by Geoffrey Chaucer.
Very slightly reduced from the original.
Executed with stick ink on handmade paper.

L'Hotel Splendide

CHARLES PEARCE
Design for use on a T-shirt.
Size of original 13" x 7½"
Courtesy of Mr Donald Bodden

This is a list of some of the better books on calligraphy:

PEN LETTERING – Ann Camp
CALLIGRAPHY TODAY – Heather Child
CALLIGRAPHY FOR THE BEGINNER – Tom Gourdie
THE STORY OF WRITING – Donald Jackson
WRITING AND ILLUMINATING AND LETTERING, – Edward Johnston
THE ART OF LETTERING WITH THE BROAD PEN – Byron J·Macdonald
MODERN SCRIBES & LETTERING ARTISTS – an anthology of the
            finest contemporary calligraphy and lettering.
ITALIC CALLIGRAPHY AND HANDWRITING – Lloyd J·Reynolds
THE IRENE WELLINGTON COPYBOOK – Irene Wellington